DOWNERS GROVE PUBLIC LIBRARY

3 1191 00932 9665

P9-CQW-289

J 530.8 ROB
Robbins, Ken.
For good measure

JUNIOR ROOM
DOWNERS GROVE PUBLIC LIBRARY

APR 16 2010

Downers Grove Public Library
1050 Curtiss St.
Downers Grove, IL 60515
(630) 960-1200
www.downersgrovelibrary.org

WITHDRAWN
DOWNERS GROVE PUBLIC LIBRARY GAYLORD

FOR GOOD MEASURE

THE WAYS WE SAY HOW MUCH, HOW FAR, HOW HEAVY, HOW BIG, HOW OLD

FOR GOOD MEASURE

THE WAYS WE SAY HOW MUCH, HOW FAR, HOW HEAVY, HOW BIG, HOW OLD

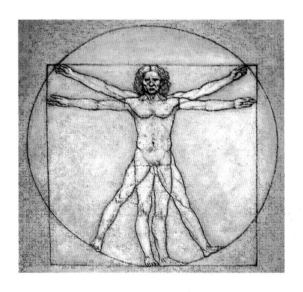

KEN ROBBINS

A Neal Porter Book
Roaring Brook Press
New York

Text copyright © 2010 by Ken Robbins

All photographs copyright © 2010 by Ken Robbins unless otherwise noted

A Neal Porter Book

Published by Flash Point, an imprint of Roaring Brook Press

Roaring Brook Press is a division of Holtzbrinck Publishing Holdings Limited Partnership

175 Fifth Avenue, New York, New York 10010

www.roaringbrookpress.com

All rights reserved

Distributed in Canada by H. B. Fenn and Company Ltd.

Cataloging-in-Publication Data is on file at the Library of Congress

ISBN: 978-1-59643-344-1

Roaring Brook Press books are available for special promotions and premiums.

For details contact: Director of Special Markets, Holtzbrinck Publishers.

First Edition April 2010

Book design by Ken Robbins and Lilian Rosenstreich

Printed in October 2009 in China by Leo Paper, Henshan City, Guangdong Province

1 3 5 7 9 8 6 4 2

To Irene Tulley, a teacher with boundless energy and deep love of learning, and to the countless students she has inspired over the years.

ACKNOWLEDGMENTS

The following people went out of their way to be helpful in the making of this book, and I am grateful to them all: Roger Cooper; Tim Lee; Pamela Williams; Lydia Salant; Lorraine Dusky; Paul Hamilton; Charles Waller; Richard J. Sawyer; and Jeff, of Trees by Jeff.

ART CREDITS

"Vitruvian Man" on page 3 by Leonardo da Vinci
Bridge photo on page 17 by Andreas Praefcke
Race track photo on page 18 by Andrea Hancock
Deep space photo on page 21 courtesy NASA
Photo of oxen plowing on page 22 by Luke Birky, from the Tom Lehman Collection,
courtesy of the Luis Muñoz Marín Foundation, San Juan, PR
Aerial photos (football field on page 23 and shoreline on page 24) by Doug Kuntz
Satellite photo on page 24 courtesy of U.S. Department of Agriculture
Photo of drachma coins on page 30 courtesy of Hixenbaugh Ancient Art
Earth from space on page 48 courtesy NASA
All other photos by Ken Robbins

INTRODUCTION

Certain words and phrases that we use to describe things are just not very specific: "lots," "scads," and "many," for instance, or pairs of opposites like "far" and "near," "big" and "small," "light" and "heavy," "new" and "old." With words like that it's hard to know exactly what somebody means. Sometimes it doesn't matter so much, but when it does matter, we need standards of measurement that we can compare things to—units we can all agree on.

Most of the units of measure we use today are pretty old. How old, you ask? Well, we know that the Earth has revolved around the Sun at least 7,000 times since carpenters first used the cubit to measure length. According to the Bible, Noah was told to build his Ark 300 cubits long. Now, the cubit is not a very precise measurement, but then in general the further back you go in history, the less exact the units of measurement were. Of course they came to be more exact as time went by, because people's needs changed. To sell and trade with people far away, you need to have standards that are understood by both parties. And modern science requires standards that are very, very precise indeed.

Long ago it was often kings and queens who simply declared how the various units of measurement should be determined. These days such things are more often decided by a legislature, a special commission, or else by international treaty. In spite of that, or perhaps because of it, measurements can be a bit confusing.

So here are some facts about units of measure, and how they compare to one another—and some pictures to help you get an idea of "how much" each one is.

A FEW WORDS
ABOUT THE METRIC SYSTEM

The units of measure in this book come mostly from British and European traditions that arrived here with the early settlers, sometimes changing slightly in the ways that people used and defined them. Their origins are ancient and their stories are fascinating.

It should be said, however, that these days, most of the world uses the metric system, a newer and perhaps more practical system based on decimal numbers. That means all the units can be neatly divided or multiplied by ten. In theory, this country is attempting to switch over to the metric system, but people are slow to change. In this book I've included metric equivalents (indicated parenthetically in orange) of most measures that are mentioned.

In the metric system, the basic unit of length is the meter—39.37 inches or just a bit more than a yard. One-hundredth of a meter is a centimeter (2.54 centimeters to the inch); a thousandth of a meter is a millimeter. The kilometer is 1,000 meters or just under two-thirds of a mile.

In the metric system the basic unit of liquid volume is the liter, which is just a bit more than a quart (1.056 liquid quarts, to be precise). There are, of course, centiliters ($^1/_{1000}$ of a liter), deciliters ($^1/_{10}$ of the liter), and kiloliters (1,000 liters).

Finally, there is the basic unit of weight in the metric system, which is the gram—just over one-third of an ounce. A kilogram is 1,000 grams (2.21 pounds). A centigram is 100 grams (just over 3.52 ounces).

Interestingly, although ten years is called a decade, one hundred years is a century, and one thousand years is a millennium, there is no basic metric unit for time.

The words "metric," and "meter" both come from the Greek word *metron*, which means "measurement."

Lengths measure the size of objects. Distances measure how far apart objects are. The same units of measurement can be used for each, but it's usually (though not always) the smaller ones that are used for lengths and the larger ones that are used for distance. Smaller units of length are mostly based on parts of the body. Longer units of distance are mostly based on actions. You'll see what I mean.

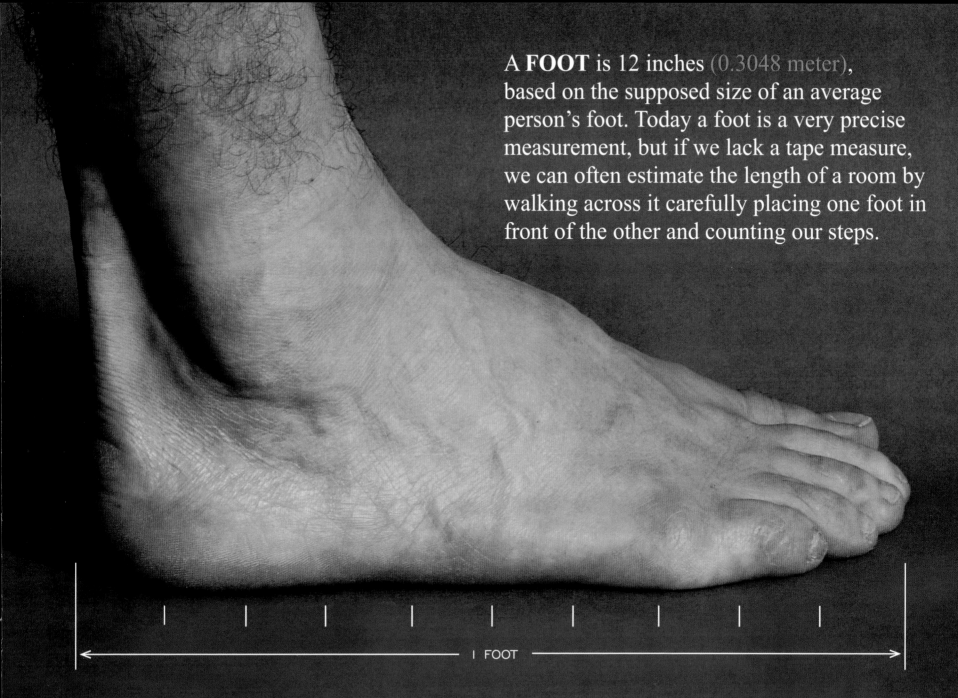

A **FOOT** is 12 inches (0.3048 meter), based on the supposed size of an average person's foot. Today a foot is a very precise measurement, but if we lack a tape measure, we can often estimate the length of a room by walking across it carefully placing one foot in front of the other and counting our steps.

I FOOT

An **INCH** is one twelfth of a foot (2.54 centimeters). Its name comes from *uncia*, which means one-twelfth in the Latin language. One twelfth of what? In this case, a foot, of course. *Uncia* is also the source of our word *ounce*—more about that later.

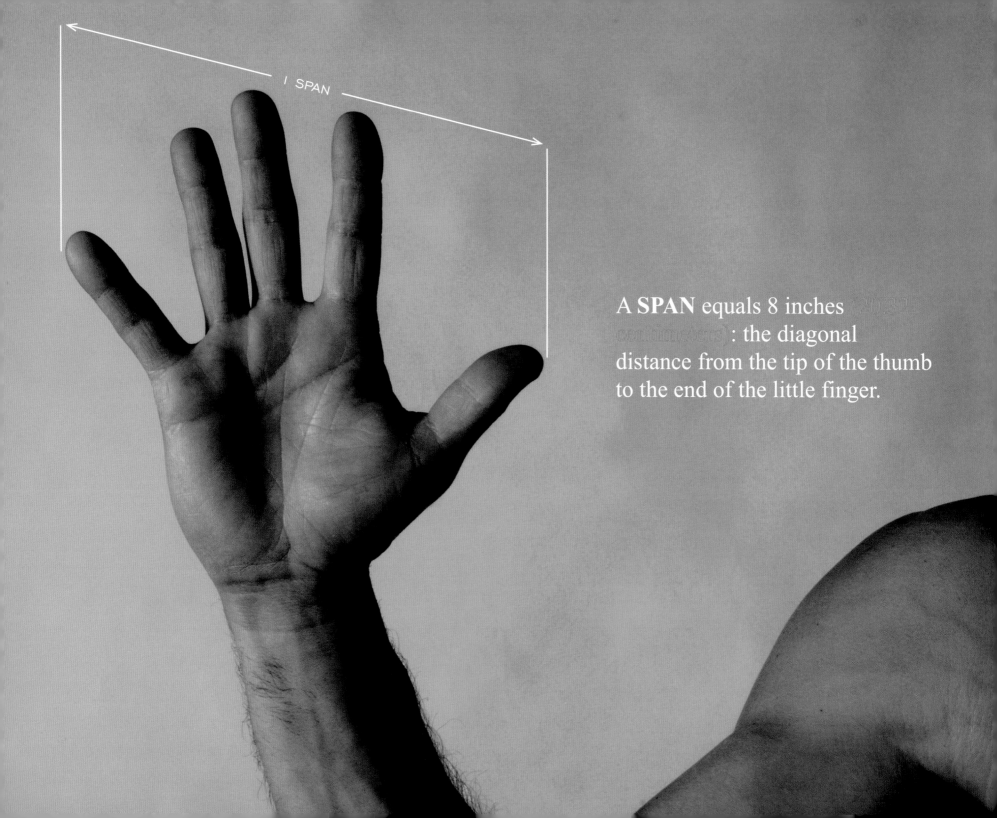

I SPAN

A **SPAN** equals 8 inches : the diagonal distance from the tip of the thumb to the end of the little finger.

I HAND

A **HAND** equals 4 inches (10.16 centimeters): the width of a male human palm (not including the thumb). These days it's used mostly to indicate the height of horses or ponies.

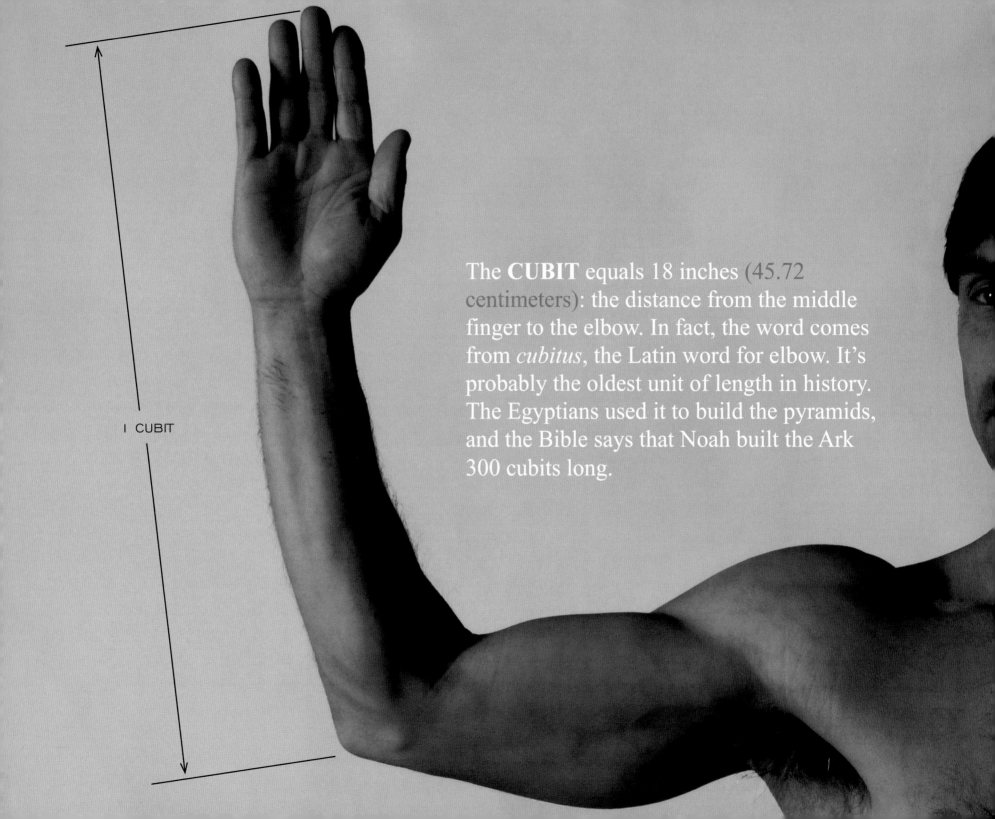

I CUBIT

The **CUBIT** equals 18 inches (45.72 centimeters): the distance from the middle finger to the elbow. In fact, the word comes from *cubitus*, the Latin word for elbow. It's probably the oldest unit of length in history. The Egyptians used it to build the pyramids, and the Bible says that Noah built the Ark 300 cubits long.

I YARD

A **YARD** is 3 feet (0.9144 meter). That's double the length of a cubit. At one time, a yard was defined as the distance from the tip of the nose to the thumb with the arm stretched out.

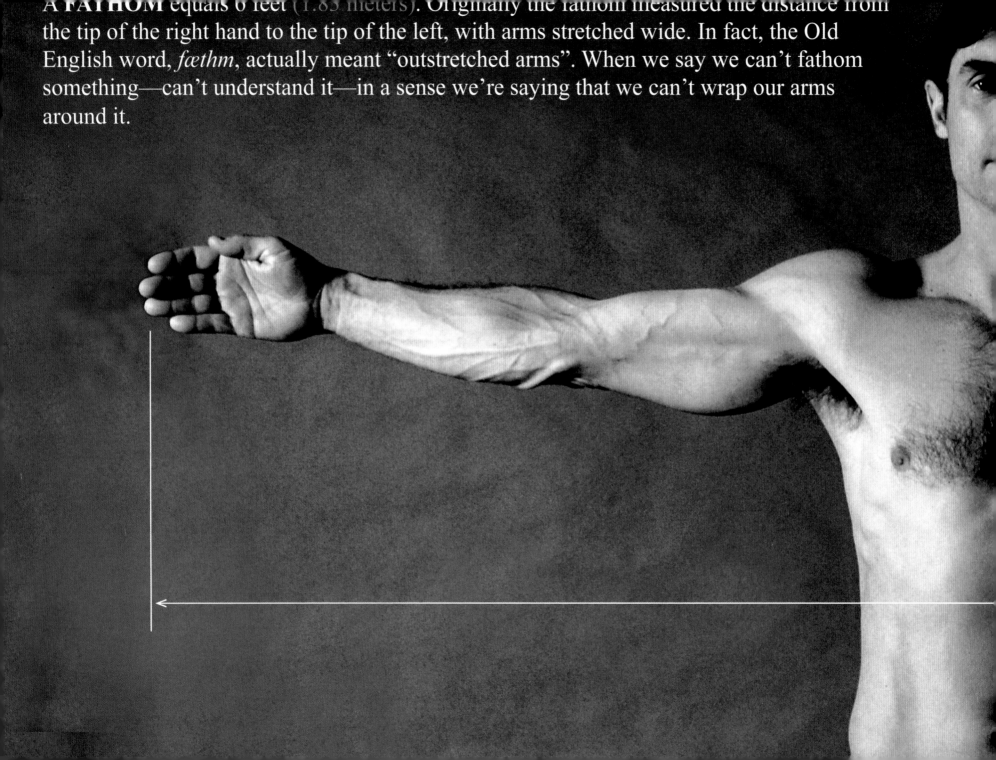

A **FATHOM** equals 6 feet (1.85 meters). Originally the fathom measured the distance from the tip of the right hand to the tip of the left, with arms stretched wide. In fact, the Old English word, *fæthm*, actually meant "outstretched arms". When we say we can't fathom something—can't understand it—in a sense we're saying that we can't wrap our arms around it.

I FATHOM

A **MILE** is 5,280 feet or 1,760 yards (1,609 meters). A good runner can go a mile in under 4 minutes. It takes an average person about 20 to walk that far. Our word *mile* comes from the Latin phrase, *mille passus*, which means 1,000 paces.

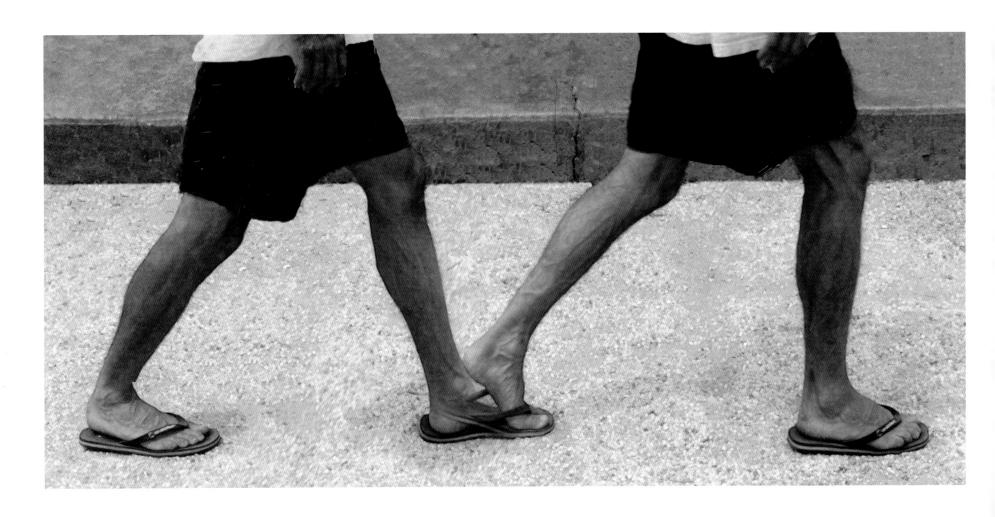

A pace, by the way, is TWO steps—left and right!

I MILE

The Verrazano-Narrows Bridge spans the Hudson River

I FURLONG

A **FURLONG** is 220 yards or one-eighth of a mile (201.168 meters). It's name means "long furrow"—the straight distance a farmer would plow with a team of oxen before turning them round for another row. Today it is used only to indicate the length of a horse race. A 7-furlong race is 1,540 yards—almost precisely seven-eighths of a mile.

A **ROD** is 5 ½ yards or 16 ½ feet (5.0292 meters). It was originally a stick used to prod the oxen that were plowing a field.

I LEAGUE (3 MILES)

A **LEAGUE** is 3 miles (4.828 kilometers)—once thought to be the distance a man could walk in an hour. In fairy tales there are sometimes references to "Seven League Boots"—magical boots that allow the wearer to travel seven leagues in a single step (that would be 21 miles in fairy steps).

A **LIGHT-YEAR** is the distance light will travel in a year. The Sun is 93,000,000 miles from Earth, yet its light takes just 18 minutes to get here. Imagine how much farther that same light would travel in a whole year.

No need to imagine, actually, the answer is just under 5.9 trillion miles (9.5 trillion kilometers). Needless to say, this measurement is used only to measure distances in outer space.

Sirius, the Dog Star, is the brightest star in the night sky, in part because it's so "close."

How close?

Sirus is 8.6 light years away, which is to say (in round figures) about 50,740,000,000,000 —that's well over 50 trillion miles—away.

TWO CONSTELLATIONS in the night sky: Canis Major, with the bright star, Sirius, where its collar would be, following after its master, Orion the Hunter.

AREA

Area is a measure of flat space—the floor of a room, the side of a barn, or the surface of the Earth, to name just three examples. Any measure of length or distance can be used to measure area by multiplying the width by the length. The resulting units of area are said to be squared units.

An area of land is often measured in ACRES. An acre was originally the amount of land a man and a team of oxen could plow in a day. In fact, it comes from a Middle English word *aker*, which meant "field." Today an acre is officially 4,840 square yards, or 43,560 square feet (4,046.86 square meters). The area in light green is one acre. It's very nearly 80 percent of an American football field.

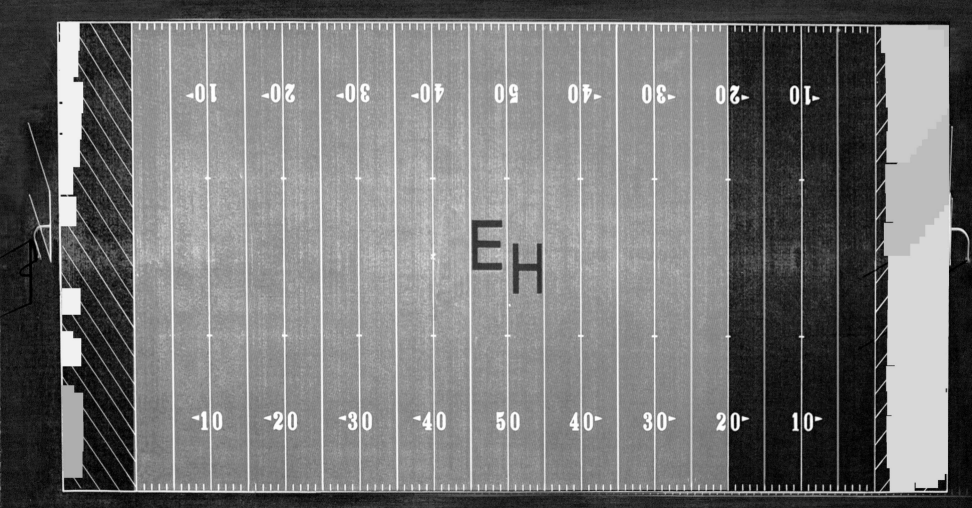

A HECTARE is a metric measure of area, equaling 10,000 square meters. There are approximately 2.5 hectares in an acre.

A **SECTION** is 640 acres (258.9 hectares) or one square mile (that's one mile wide and one mile long). In the Midwest, roads were often laid out along section lines, and this aerial photo shows sections of land outlined by roads running north and south, east and west. You can see two full sections here. The yellow square in the upper left-hand corner represents approximately one acre.

WEIGHTS

Gravity is a force that pulls objects together. Because the Earth is a large object with great mass, it exerts a lot of gravity, pulling much smaller things, like people, balls, and cars, downward. The strength of that force depends on the mass of the object, or the number of atoms contained in the object—and we call that strength weight.

A **POUND** is 16 ounces (453.592 grams or a bit less than .5 kilogram). Its name comes from the Latin word *pondus*, but that just meant weight. *Libra* was the real unit of measure. The Latin phrase *libra pondo* meant a "*libra* of weight." Over the years people began to call it a pound, but it's still abbreviated "lb." for libra. Not coincidentally, the Latin word for the scales used to measure weight was also libra—and so we have the astrological sign called Libra: The Scales.

According to regulations, a soccer ball must weigh between 14 and 16 ounces. This one weighs exactly 16 ounces, which equals…1 pound.

An **OUNCE** is one-sixteenth of a pound (28.35 grams). Its name comes from *uncia,* the same Latin word that gave us "inch." It actually means "one-twelfth" in Latin, but at some point in history it was decided to divide a pound into sixteen parts, rather than twelve. Still, the name stuck, and we call it an ounce.

Coins are usually measured in grams, a metric unit of weight, but if you can imagine the weight of five (modern) quarters in your hand, that's pretty close to an ounce of weight. 99.75 percent close, in fact.

Don't confuse an ounce of weight with a fluid ounce, by the way. A fluid ounce of water weighs pretty nearly one ounce, but a fluid ounce of other things (like mercury, for instance) may weigh much more.

A **TON** is 2,000 pounds (907.18 kilograms)—about the weight of a large buffalo or a small car.

The word comes from *tun*, which was and still is a cask or wooden barrel used for holding, and especially shipping wine in large quantities—256 gallons, in most cases, which would weigh (approximately) 2,000 pounds.

Once upon a time a person might have picked up any handy rock or stone and used it to judge the weight of other things by comparison. Over the years the idea got standardized, and today a **STONE** is 14 pounds (6.4 kilograms). As a unit of measure, it's kind of old-fashioned, but in older books (especially ones from Great Britain) you may see the weight of a man or a large animal given in stone. Despite using metric measurements for nearly everything else, the British still use stone to measure body weight. (In this special case only, the plural of stone is…stone. A man weighing 168 pounds, for example, may be said to weigh 12 stone.)

A **DRAM** is a sixteenth of an ounce (1.77 grams)—sometimes still spelled (as it was in the past) "drachm." It gets its name, though, from a small Greek coin called the drachma, which in the past people sometimes used as a standard of weight as well as of money. The drachma goes back approximately 1,500 years, and until recently (when the Euro became official) was the official currency of Greece.

Actual size of coins

A **CARAT** is a very small unit of weight used exclusively to measure diamonds and other gems. Today it is defined as two-tenths of a gram. The interesting thing about it, though, is that its name comes from the carob seed (of which you are looking at many). Long ago people thought that carob seeds were so uniform that they would make a good standard of weight.

LIQUID MEASURES

Liquids change shape easily, so a quart of liquid will fit into any container big enough to hold it—whether tall and thin, short and wide, square, cylindrical, or even shaped (more or less) like a leaf.

A **DROP** is the smallest amount
of liquid that drips (or drops)
in whole form as it falls. The
word is usually used carelessly
to mean any very small quantity
of a liquid, but in cooking it is
considered $\frac{1}{76}$ of a teaspoon.

There are 3 **TEASPOONS** (approximately 5 milliliters) in a **TABLESPOON** (about 15 milliliters), and 2 tablespoons (about 30 milliliters) in a fluid ounce. Both are named after common utensils, which generally hold approximately those amounts. The word *spoon* comes from an Old English word that meant "chip of wood."

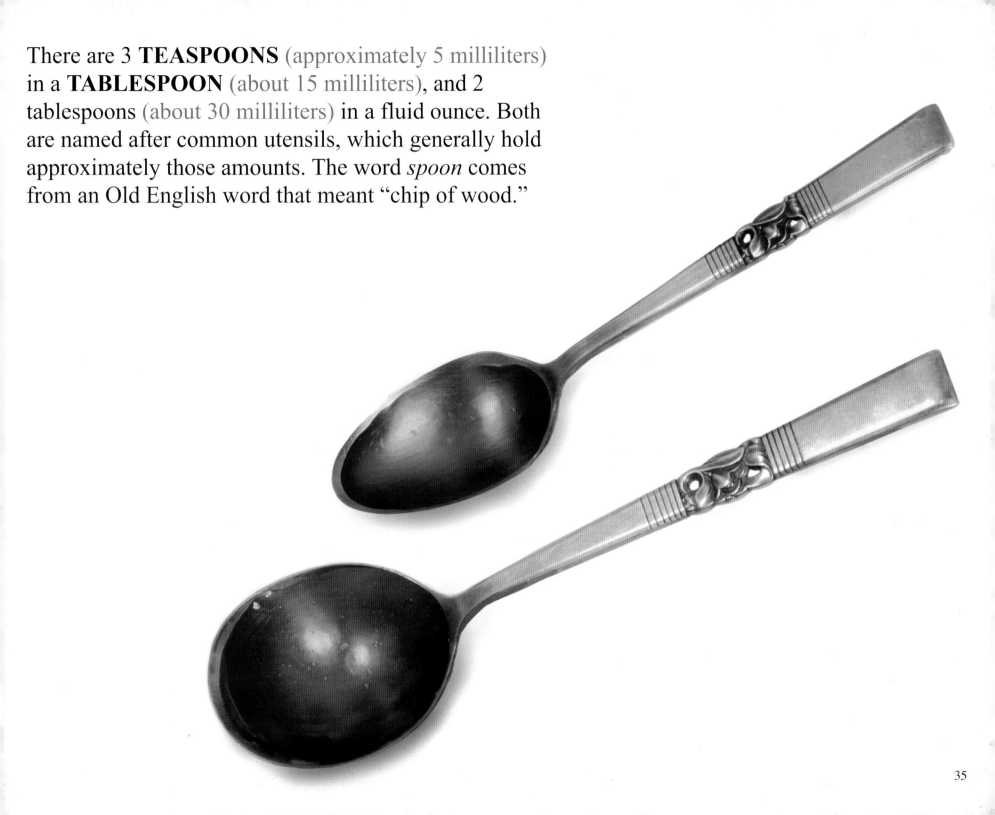

A **FLUID OUNCE** is 2 tablespoons of liquid (almost 30 milliliters). The word, once again, comes from the Latin, *uncia*, meaning a twelfth part (remember inches and feet). Somewhere along the line, though, it was changed to one-sixteenth of a pint.

A **CUP** is half a pint, one-fourth of a quart, 8 ounces or 16 tablespoons (237 milliliters). The word comes from a Latin word, *cuppa*, which means a drinking vessel. Actually, our word *cup* also means a drinking vessel: The teacup below, however, is holding exactly one cup of tea.

A **PINT** (just under half a liter) equals to half a quart, or one-eighth of a gallon, or 16 ounces. No one seems to remember where the name came from.

A **QUART** (just a bit less than a liter) equals 2 pints or one-fourth of a gallon. In fact, its name comes from the Latin word *quartus*, which literally means one-fourth or a quarter (of a gallon).

A **GALLON** is 4 quarts, 8 pints, 16 cups, or 128 ounces (3.75 liters). The word comes from an old French word, *galun*, a measure for wine. Lots of liquids are sold by the gallon—particularly gasoline.

This is a quarter (no pun intended)

A **BARREL** is a cylindrical container used
to hold a substantial amount of liquid.
In the past they were generally made of
staves of wood held together with bands
of metal. The artisans who made barrels
were called coopers. Modern barrels may
be made of wood, metal, or plastic, and
their size depends on what they are used
to hold. A barrel of oil holds 42 gallons, a
barrel of beer 36 gallons, and one of wine
31 gallons.

DRY CAPACITIES

Things that are dry (not liquid) fit together roughly, with spaces in between the pieces, so dry measures are a little less exact than liquid measures. Things like apples, potatoes, or strawberries are often sold in dry measures.

A **PECK** of potatoes. Four pecks in a bushel.

A **BUSHEL** of apples.

A **PINT** of strawberries. There are 16 pints in a peck.

A **CORD** of firewood is a stack of wood 4 feet high, and 4 feet wide, and 8 feet long. It got its name because the stack was originally measured with a length of cord.

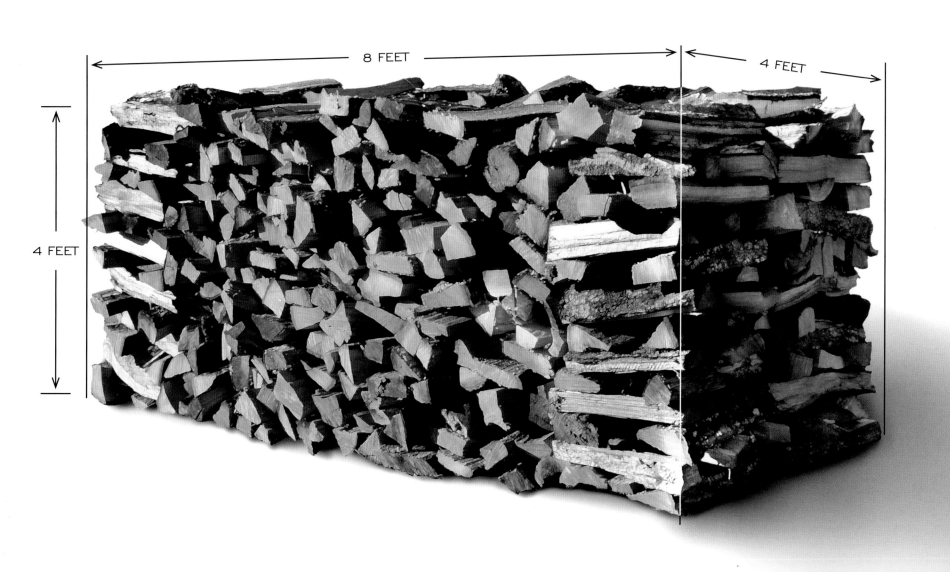

8 FEET

4 FEET

4 FEET

TIME

Time is the stuff that slips away, never to return. You can't see it or touch it, but you can measure it. It's the interval between one event and another—between one winter and the next (a year), one heartbeat and the next (a second).

A **YEAR** is the time it takes the Earth to revolve around the Sun—precisely 365 ¼ days. That's why, since we have only 365 days in our calendar, we need a leap day every four years. Like the month, it's a natural unit of time based on observation, and it includes the cycle of the four seasons.

The **SECOND** is the smallest measure of time that we normally consider. It corresponds very roughly to the time of a heartbeat. Its name comes from the Latin phrase: *pars minuta secunda*—which means the second small part (of a day). Why the second part?

Because the first small part of the day is the **MINUTE**, from the Latin phrase *pars minuta prima*—the first small part (of the day). A related word, spelled the same but pronounced differently (MY-NOOT) is still used to mean "small."

There are 60 seconds in a minute, and there are 60 minutes in an **HOUR**; one twenty-fourth of a day. The Greek word from which it comes, *hora*, originally meant any relatively limited amount of time, and we sometimes still use it that way. (If we say, "This is my hour of need," we don't mean one hour of need, but something more like general time.)

IT'S TIME

A **DAY** is 24 hours long. That's the time it takes the Earth to make one complete rotation as it spins around. It is related to an ancient Sanskrit word meaning to burn (*dah*), because it originally meant just the hours of sunlight. Later it came to have the additional meaning of the 24 hours from midnight to midnight.

A **WEEK** is 7 days. There are 52 weeks in a year. The cycle of 7 days was first used in the Jewish calendar and since then has been adopted by Christians, Muslims, and other cultures, as well. The name comes from the Old English word *wiku*.

FORTNIGHT is short for "fourteen nights"—two weeks' time. It's not used much anymore, but you will sometimes read it in literature from past centuries.

A **MONTH** varies in this country from 28 to 31 days. It's related to the word *moon*, and it roughly measures the time it takes the moon to revolve around the Earth. There are twelve months in a year.

The phases of the moon in one month

A **CENTURY** is 100 years. Named for *centum*, the Latin word for one hundred. Though some people have lived longer, a 100-year-old person is a very old person indeed.

A **MILLENNIUM** is 1,000 years. It's named for the Latin word *mille* meaning 1,000. We have recently entered the third millennium since the year one, but that's only in our system of counting. Time itself is so vast it makes the mind hurt to try to think of it all.

AN **EON** (also spelled AEON) is the largest division of time. In geology and astronomy it is used loosely to mean any huge and more or less unimaginable span of time. For example, the current best guess for the age of the Earth is 4.5 billion years—an eon for sure. From a Greek word, *aion*, which means age or eternity…

…something that really can't be measured at all.

7,926.41 MILES

3 1191 00932 9665